Loss in Brooklyn

Aaliyah Hall

ROYAL MEDIA
PUBLISHING

Royal Media and Publishing
P. O. Box 4321
Jeffersonville, IN 47131
502-802-5385
http://royamediaandpublishing.com
royalmediapublishing@gmail.com

Cover Design: Elite Cover Designs

ISBN-13: 978-0-9987154-6-9

Printed in the United States of America

To My Mommy,

Claudia Khietha Hall

TABLE OF CONTENTS

Chapter 1

Mommy is Gone!

The screams of mommy woke me from my sleep.

I can clearly see mommy yelling and screaming, "My mommy's dead! My mommy's dead!"

We had lived in a small one-bedroom apartment in Brooklyn New York on Willmore Street. I quickly jumped up through the covers back and out of bed I ran in to see what was wrong. I had never seen that kind of pain on my mommy's face before. She was screaming and crying. I was young and didn't know what to do. I was seemingly helpless. The tears quickly fell my eyes and I am watching the pain of my mother. I remember mommy and I crying and hugging each other while we cried. What happens next? What do we do now?

The next morning, I woke up with my mommy's loving arms around me. At first, I had thought it was all a dream. I laid there wondering was it a dream? Even though my mommy was holding me, I could tell by her spirit that it wasn't a dream, it was real. My grandmother was gone. After I was awake, mommy began preparing our things for our trip to Virginia. Yes, my grandmother lived in Virginia. A long way from New York and the trip would be even longer this time because of the reason for the trip.

I remembered that it was so cold outside that I could see my breath, but mommy seemed to notice the cold at all. Mommy was walking around numb to it all. It was like she didn't feel the cold. The inside of mommy's body reflected the outside, nothing but cold.

The train ride to Virginia seemed like it took forever. Mommy wasn't talking much and she couldn't stop the tears from falling from her eyes. It made me sad to see my mommy crying. I wished there had been something that I could have done to stop her tears and pain.

Once we arrived in Virginia, we were greeted by family and friends. I remember walking into my grandmother's house. It didn't seem real because grandma or Grandma as I called her wasn't there. She wasn't there to greet me. She always loved calling me 'my lil Lele.' I was younger but I remembered seeing everyone in the family there in the house to greet us. The house was no longer the fun, familiar place. The building was the same but it was now a new experience and a new feeling of empty which I had never felt before here in my grandmother's house in Virginia. Such a tragedy. All of the pain, agony and loss. But this was only just the beginning. How did we get here? Let's go back so that we can truly go forward.

Chapter 2

Back to the Beginning

Mommy was from New York with both of her parents. Mommy was about 5'8 very tall and slim. She always kept her hair in her favorite hairstyle which was long black hair with Chinese bangs. Mommy had a great personality. She loved to get dress and go out with her friends. We lived New York all of my life. I remember when mommy used to send me to the corner stores for groceries or to get seafood. My mommy and I loved seafood and Caribbean food. She would always get curry goat roti or the rice and peas with the goat and always had to eat that or shrimp whenever we got take out or to go for dinner. Mommy was working as a security guard at the time in Downtown Brooklyn in New York. She loved that job. At the time, we travelled back and forth from NEW YORK to Virginia. We travelled to Virginia to visit Grandma because she was sick at the time. Grandma was fighting for her life. She was dealing with and fighting colon cancer. Cancer is no joke. In Virginia, my mom was known for her deep city accent. Virginia in comparison to New York is the country. Mommy was known as the girl from NEW YORK. Mommy loved to shop and you would never see mommy in the same outfit more than once. That's just how she was. She loved to have on something new every day. My mommy had a best friend in Virginia named Tina. When you saw one you saw the other. They were more like sisters than friends. Tina is my God mommy. She has always been around me since I was born. She is like my second mom.

She always made sure me and mommy didn't want for a nothing. Mommy made sure she called Tina to come get us so we can all hang out when we came to Virginia. I remember when the three of us would go to the park. Mommy would play with me at the park. I would climb into her lap and we would swing. Virginia was totally different than New York. In New York, I didn't like to be outside much and neither did she because we were from the city and didn't like the Virginia bugs. Neither of us like bugs. Back in NEW YORK, we didn't have many bugs but there was certainly a rat and roach problem that came along with the city life. The smell of trash and old beer or malt liquor bottles on the ground outside as well as thrown on the floor in the big tall buildings. When you see the trash, you knew you were back in NEW YORK. NEW YORK is a fast-paced life. Everything is fast paced. People in New York walk and talk fast. They keep it moving. People from the city aren't always friendly like in Virginia. People talk about people in New York not being nice but that is truth not fiction. New Yorkers have attitudes and that is how you have to be in NEW YORK. It is survival. In NEW YORK, there is a store on each corner. I remember walking down to the hair store that was down in the street. I would go to the hair store so mommy can do my hair. When I had left over change from the hair store, I would buy big bamboo earrings that were very popular back the 90's. I would wear my earrings when and where my mommy would wear her earrings when she went out. She would look me and just laugh. Mommy was my best friend. She was more of a friend to me than a hard disciplinarian. She never yelled at me or gave me whippings. I remember when I was 7. I had a knife in my hand and was sticking it into the electrical outlet to get something out. That time she yelled at me, "What are you doing you can get electrocuted!"

At that time, we were living on Williammore St in Apartment 2B. I would always play outside with the neighbor's kids. I would ride my bike and skate up and down in the hallways in the apartment building. Mommy would always come outside to check up on me. I remember one day this girl was being mean to me and wasn't sharing the toys that were mine. I ran upstairs to our apartment with tears falling from my eyes. When I walked in mommy asked me, "what is wrong?" I remember telling her the girl from down in the hall was being mean to me. My mom immediately went down the stairs and said something to the girl and told her "you can go get your mama if you want!" My mama didn't play about her child.

Chapter 3

Season of Loss 2004

Ma, my mother's mom was 49 at the time of her death. It was the fall of the year. The leaves had changed and so was our lives. I didn't quite understand death at the time. I just knew she was gone and I was gonna see her again. Ma had been sick for a while. Mommy told me she had colon cancer a while back when I used to go visit Ma during the holidays and for the summer. I loved coming to visit my Aunt RiRi along with Ma and Da. Da was my mom's stepfather. I called him Da. Da was Ma's husband and she met him when she came to live to Virginia and she had Aunt RiRi. Aunt RiRi is my mom youngest sister. I loved to be with my Aunt RiRi especially when I lost Ma. Aunt RiRi would always try and put a smile on my face and make me laugh, When Ma died, I felt as if everything changed. Mommy was sad and so was Aunt RiRi and Da. I remember going up to the house thinking Ma was still around then. I realized she isn't here in New York any more. It took a while for the family to get over Ma's death. I realize now that you never really get over death. The thought that a person you loved the most is gone is something that will always be with you no matter how long you live. Mommy had a hard time dealing with Ma's death. She blamed herself a lot. She wished she could go back in time and change how things were. I was still little at the time. I tried my best to keep mommy calm and happy but for some reason that didn't seem to work as much. Mommy went out more each weekend because she tried to hide the pain that her mom was gone. Mommy tried to make things right by working and doing her best to take care of me, but her heart was empty. I didn't quite understand her pain until one day, I found myself in her shoes. The feeling of being empty without your mom is the worst feeling.

Two months had passed and its Dec. 24th Christmas Eve like most kids my age I was excited to get my gifts tomorrow. Mommy went out with her friends that night Linda and Kia. These were mommy's friends. Linda had 2 kids, a boy and girl. Kia had 5 kids. They always would come over and I play with there, at

Kia's house with her kids while they all went out.

Mommy was so ready to get dressed to leave to go out. I loved watching mommy do her hair as I sat on the toilet. I watched her begin to get dress for her night out with her friends. I remember that night like it was yesterday and always will. Before mommy left, I asked her to bring me my favorite toy that I already knew she got me for Christmas. I remember crying and begging mommy "Please stay home with me and don't go out please!" Mommy said, "It's okay. I'll be right back. I'm coming back."

As mommy closed the door behind her. I ran to the window and watched her walk down in the street. She was dancing and laughing ready to have a good old time at the club with her friends. Who would of thought that would be the last time I would see my mommy alive? The next morning it was Christmas. I woke up and saw mommy bought that toy that I had asked for right next to me. As I got out of bed, I went to thank mommy but mommy wasn't there. I was confused because mommy wouldn't just leave me somewhere and not call. I saw that she did come back. I had my toy but where is mommy??? I walked into the next bedroom and saw Linda in her bed.

I asked her, "Where is my mommy? Where did she go?"

I was told mommy left with a friend who worked with her who dropped her off at another friend's house. Linda called mommy at least 100 times and so did I. A week had passed and mommy was still missing with no phone calls or text messages from New York or anybody. We all started to get worried 'cause it wasn't like mommy to be gone this long. Especially not call me, her daughter Aaliyah! I was worried.

Where is mommy? I wanted my mommy. I sat there and cried. I cried for days because my mommy was missing and nobody saw or heard from her. Me and Linda was outside putting up flyers around the neighborhood asking people have they see my mom. At 10 years old, I was out trying to find my mom. I was staying with my mommy's childhood friend. I had stayed with her and her daughter so I could still go to school until they figured out where my mommy was located. A few days have passed now, I was sitting in class. The school principal pulled me out of class and asked me to come to the main office. As I was walking down in the hallway, all I could do is think that yes mommy is back wherever she has been in all of this time. When I got to the office, I noticed my dad's mom, my other grandma and Grandma Lora was in the office. I was puzzled because I'm wondering why is she here and not mommy. The tears started falling from my eyes.

I had asked, "why are you here to get me from school?"

Grandma Lora said, "Aaliyah you have to come stay with me for a while."

I was so upset and confused because all I knew and thought was my mom didn't want to come get me? I didn't want to go and stay with my dad's mom. I just wanted my mom. Where is my mommy? My dad's mom took care of me at the time her son, which is my dad is away in jail. He has been in jail since I was 2 years old. Since he's been gone it was just me and grandma. The ride back to Long Island NEW YORK Roosevelt was a long ride and it took forever to get there. All I could think about is mommy. 'Please come to get me. Where are you?'

Here it is the next morning. I woke up and just laid in the bed. I do that a lot when I don't want to be bothered. Grandma Lora called me to come in to her room. As I walked down the hall into Grandma Lora's room, I opened her door and saw her face. All I can see is the pain in her eyes. Grandma Lora had been crying but I didn't know what is wrong. She said Aaliyah I have to tell you something, the cops found your mom.

I said, "Really let's go get her."

I missed mommy so much. The tears started falling from her face. She said, "No Aaliyah your mom is gone. She has been murdered." My heart dropped I felt myself starting to get sick. I didn't quite understand. The tears started falling down my face as I began to cry. I literally cried all night. I cried for days. Now I totally understand the feeling that mommy had when her mom, my other Grandma had died. I felt empty like a part of me is gone. My mommy was my best friend, my dad and my everything. Now she's gone!

Mommy's funeral was on New Year's Eve. New Year's Eve was also her grandfather's birthday. Mommy death took a toll on everyone. We had just buried my grandma, her mother 2 months earlier, now my mommy. This couldn't be real. I felt like I was in a movie. Mommy was murdered. I just couldn't believe something like this just happen to her. I just didn't quite understand. I wanted Aunt RiRi. I needed Aunt RiRi to be here for me. We needed each other to get through this. I wanted to live with Aunt RiRi in Culpeper, Virginia. I couldn't be with her because she was going away soon off to college to play softball.

I remember seeing Uncle AG at the funeral. He was tall, slim, and had pretty waves in his hair like his sister grandma did. AG worked for the NEW YORK Police Department at the time. He was determined to find my mommy killers. Uncle AG was on channel Fox 5 news trying to find out if someone knew anything about my mom's death to come forward to help solve my mommy's murder. Uncle AG made sure I was ok. He and my mommy didn't have the best relationship but at the end, we were family. He wanted justice for our family. Most importantly he wanted just for me especially. Mommy's murder was all over the news, in newspapers and on America's Most Wanted. Grandma Lora called me into the room later that afternoon to watch the news story about my mommy's case. Uncle AG was on tv asking people to come forward. Uncle AG was sick himself. He had sickle cell disease but he was still fighting for his own health and life as well as justice for my mommy's life.

He was so upset that he was crying on tv. I remember him saying, "Whatever coward did this to my niece Claudia will pay." He was determined to get justice. After watching the news about my mom, everything seemed so unreal. I still couldn't believe my mom was gone and wasn't coming back for the longest. I didn't want to believe she was gone. I kept telling myself she's not gone maybe she just ran away. Always felt as if she would walk through the door with her big smile on her face. I knew that was impossible. As a kid that's what I thought and knew that's what I wanted. Grandma Lora began explaining everything to me about my mommy's murder. I remember sitting on her bed with her flower bed spread. She looked at me and started crying because she couldn't get her words out. The more she cried the more I got worried. I just couldn't believe something like that had happened. It was like I was part of a *Law and Order* episode or on the *I.D. Channel*.

Chapter 4
The Toughest Days of My Life

Living with my dad's mom, Grandma Lora was a challenge for me. I really didn't want to live with her at the time. I cried so much I just wanted my mommy. As mentioned before, at the age of 2, my dad went to jail due to selling drugs. I visited him from time to time with his mom. She was taking care of him until he came home which would have been when I was 15 years old. Grandma Lora tried to keep me busy and keep my mind off things, especially about my mommy. She took me shopping every weekend or movies just so I'm staying busy. She spoiled me a lot and got me everything and anything that I wanted. I used to love the show *That's so Raven* on *Disney Channel*. I remember her taking me to the store to get all the seasons on DVD. I was so happy when I got the DVDs because I loved that show. When it was time to start school again, it was a little hard. I didn't want to go back to school anymore. I didn't want to do anything since mommy has been gone. I didn't talk much, wasn't as happy and I stayed to myself. Apart of me was gone and I felt empty without my mommy. My dad's mom tried counseling for me inside of school and private sessions outside of school but nothing worked. Nobody understood my pain and emptiness unless you been through what I have been through. I can't express my feelings and explain how I feel to someone who doesn't understand. At this time, I was still in New York but in another part called Long Island and not any more in Brooklyn. I missed Brooklyn a lot and still do. It brings back the good and bad memories. It's the times where I used to walk to the store with mommy. I miss that so much. I lived with Grandma Lora since I was 10 yrs. She's not my real grandmother, but she's all I knew once my mom died. She took care of me. I didn't really like it too much but I had no choice. Mommy was gone and was never coming back.

When I was 14, my grandmother's son which was supposed to be my dad at the time, came home from jail. I wasn't too thrilled about the situation. I was more nervous and anxious because I didn't really know him. I knew nothing about him just that he was crazy about my mom. I wrote and saw him a few times, but once he came home things changed. We didn't get along at all and it put my Grandma Lora in a situation to where she didn't know what to do. You can't blame me for not listening to a man who I barely know. A few weeks had passed and I still wasn't talking to him. We weren't getting along. He told my Grandma Lora, "She can't be mine she acts nothing like me or anything." So, my Grandma Lora sat me down and said Aaliyah he wants to do a DNA test. Would you do it? I said sure because at this point, I honestly don't care if this man is my dad or not. I never had a dad. My mom was my everything. She did everything so I said sure why not. So, she went to call to make the appointment in the city. The city is in Manhattan which is about 1 hour 30 minutes away from Long Island depending on traffic. The car ride down, I just looked outside my window from the backseat. I'm looking up at the sky and the tall buildings and people running trying catch the metro bus. All I can think was I just want this over with. I honestly didn't care what it said and the trip to the city took forever because nobody was talking just silence. Once I got there, I was ready to get out and get this over with. They called us both to the back and swabbed our mouths on the side with a Q-tip. Once we were done there, the doctors told us he will have the results in a couple of days. A few days have passed now, I'm walking home from school with my best friend she lived on the other side of Roosevelt New York but we always walked each other to Park Avenue store to get some snacks. She would go her way and I would go mine. New York doesn't have many school buses. We walked, took the subway or bus. I was having a good day. I told Shay I would see her tomorrow at school and went on home. When I got there, I noticed my Grandma Lora's green Buick sitting there outside. I knew something was up because she normally is at work until 6 or 7 or sometime later because of her job. I would have to call her everyday when I got into the house but today I didn't. She was home and I knew something wasn't right. As I opened the gate to go into the house, I saw Taye and Cody our dogs and they started to bark and get happy when they saw me. My

Grandma Lora came to the door saying, "Come inside Aaliyah I have got to talk to you about something." She said sit down let me talk to you. She had a paper in her hand she said we got the results back and he's not your father after all. I just looked and said ok with an attitude because at this point, I don't care and I barely knew him. Who would thought from that day on things will be different? My Grandma Lora was hurt. She told me how she felt but it was nothing I can do. Do you blame me? I'm just a child and my mom isn't here to say her side, so there was nothing I can say. She was hurt and the longer I stayed the worst things got at home. Everything changed. I felt unwanted and wanted my mom that's it. I didn't care about having a dad or anything. I just wanted my mom. She was the dad I knew and mom was my best friend all in one and this was when I needed her the most . I became angrier and asked God, "Why me? Why you take the one person that I had?" I didn't care about anything else I just knew my mom was gone and I will never see her again. I went to my room and slammed the door and threw everything. I didn't ask for none of this! All I can think about is my mom. I just wanted her to come walking through my door and tell me things will be ok, but I knew that wasn't going to happen. I sat on my bed and began to write in my diary. My Grandma Lora always had me do that when I felt a need to want to talk to my mom. It worked sometimes but I still wished she was here.

Jared is the guy who I thought was my father until the age of 15. We got DNA test results and found out that he was not my father. That day I got the news that's when I experienced another huge loss. The man I thought was my father wasn't my father at all. I wasn't too hurt by it because I never had a relationship with him. After Grandma Lora sat me down at the table and told me the results. At first, I was confused but she explained everything to me. When I look back, I realize that on the day that I got the results, not only did I lose someone that was supposed to be my dad, but I lost Grandma Lora as well. Things changed between us. She used to be my best friend, but as I got older, as time went on, we grew further apart. She will always have a part in my heart no matter what the test said. We finally decided to go our separate ways.

Chapter 5
Aunt RiRi

As always, I mostly looked forward to seeing my Aunt RiRi. We are only 5 years apart in age. Although she is my mommy's sister, I always looked up to her as my older sister too. I always looked at her as an example of someone I wanted to be. Aunt RiRi was into every sport you could name. You name it, she played it. Aunt RiRi was very athletic. She has always been the favorite out of the whole bunch.

Thanksgiving break was coming up soon and I was excited to go back to North Carolina "Gates County" to see my Aunt RiRi. All I can think about is my Great Grandma's sweet tea. She made the best tea. I would always say Grandma you need to put this tea in stores it's soo good . She would say no Lele I can't do that while laughing. My great Grandma made the best things for Thanksgiving. I was so ready to eat some of her collard greens, macaroni and cheese, deep fried turkey and most importantly, she made sure she had my succotash ready for me. When I got there, she knew that was my favorite. My Grandma Lora got me a plane ticket to go see my mom's family in North Caroline. After the North Carolina visit, I will be going back to Virginia with Aunt RiRi.

I said goodbye to Grandma Lora and gave her a kiss. She told me I'll see you soon. Who would of thought that would've been the last time I would see her for a few years?

Once I got to North Carolina, I was excited about this holiday, but we were still missing my mommy and her mom, my other Grandma. So, things will be different this time. Aunt RiRi was the first person for me to see. I was ready. I haven't seen her since Grandma's funeral and she didn't come to my mommy's wake in New York because of softball. (shaking my head) Aunt RiRi was always busy with softball. Our five years apart in age gap didn't help as Aunt RiRi got older and was ready to go to college. Things weren't the same between us any more especially once my mommy died and Grandma died. A lot of things changed and those things made me want to keep to myself. People would say oh you are mean or you are this and that, but no I'm still grieving over my mother's murder. Nobody will really understand until they have gone through what I did or understand how it feels to lose your mom. She wasn't just my mom, she was my mom, dad and best friend all in one person. I tried to explain to Aunt RiRi that at the time that you lost your mom which is my Grandma you still have your dad, who has always been there since your mom died. Also, my mom wasn't sick, she was murdered. The hurt, pain and all the events that happened is much different. I have to live with knowing the people that's responsible for her death are walking free. Aunt RiRi doesn't get it. Yea you lost Grandma but at least you had SOMEONE there which was your dad. I had to change schools, move back and forth and all that comes with moving and change. Aunt RiRi will never understand my situation and what all I had to deal with. The holiday time was almost over and I was ready to go back to New York. I missed the city and the big buildings, corner stores, .25 cents chips and .50 cents pop soda. I was never a big fan of the country lifestyle and I got that from my mommy. She was always in New York and Virginia and would go back and forth, but she made sure that when she got tired of Virginia she would hop on the train or bus back to New York. She loved the city and so do I.

Chapter 6

To Claudia With Love
From Tina Your Ride
or Die and Aaliyah's
Rock and Godmother

I met Claudia Hall at the age of 14 years old. We started hanging out and getting to know each other from there. We used to go to each other's house and hang with family and friends. She was from New

York. Claudia was a young woman who was humble and loved to have fun and go out. As the years went by, we became best friends and she was my ride or die. When you saw me, you saw her and when you saw her, you saw me most of the time. We used to go to basketball games together and everybody knew her by the girl from New York. Everybody loved her accent and the way she talked. Claudia was the type of person who loved to shop. I can remember when I used to go up to her house in Culpeper and we would sit outside of her parents' place and sit and talk and talk for hrs. As the years passed by,

Claudia got pregnant and she said ok bestie you are going to be a god mother. The first thing was I thought she was playing until we went to Walmart in Culpeper and we went to the baby aisle and she said ok bestie we need to start shopping for your god child. So, we went on continuing walking. I told her I'm not buying nothing until I know it's true. Claudia had this habit that when she's telling the truth she be like call Davina (which is her mother's name) and you ask her and if I'm right you gonna buy me shrimp (not to mention Claudia loved seafood and especially shrimp.)

So, I said, "ok it's a deal."

So instead of us calling her mom, we left Walmart and went back to her mom's place. I go into the house, speak as always and before I could get it out to ask Davina was Claudia pregnant, she burst out and said "Davina would you tell my bestie I'm pregnant and Davina was like what? I said is Claudia really pregnant and she said, "Yes baby she's having a baby, she said, "Why what's wrong?"

I said I thought she was joking and we made a bet. The bet was if you said she was pregnant, I had to go buy her a pound of shrimp. So, after all of that, we went shopping and I can remember I was so excited about being a godmother. So, before you knew it, I got up and went shopping. I bought Aaliyah a car seat and a whole lot of clothes and took it to Claudia's mother's house. When I walked in Claudia said, "OMG you went overboard didn't you, getting your godchild all of this stuff."

I said, "Oh no my goddaughter ain't gonna want for nothing."

During her pregnancy Claudia would be back and forth between Culpeper and New York. We would always keep in contact even when she wasn't in Virginia. Now Claudia is almost in her ninth monthly cycle when I see her again and we met at her parent's house in Virginia. I can remember I was at her place and her mom decided she wanted to go to the store that they owned called Norman Tutt store. Me and Claudia rode with her mom and as we were leaving to head to the store Claudia kept saying she's having labor pains and Davina told me to start keeping track of how far apart they were. I was doing just that while she ran into the store. By the time she got into the store Claudia says bestie I believe my water just broke. I said are you serious and she said yes and to go get Davina. I got out of the car and ran inside and told her I believe Claudia is about to have the baby so we got back in the car and immediately took her to Culpeper hospital. We got there and they immediately took her to labor and delivery and we were in the waiting room for a while. After a while, I told her mom I had to leave and to keep me posted. Later on, they sent her to Charlottesville, Virginia and that is where my goddaughter was born. Claudia was mad because I wasn't there when my goddaughter Aaliyah was born. I got there later because I was at work.

I remember walking and seeing Aaliyah's face and her mom said, "You want to hold her?"

I said sure. I'm sitting in Claudia's hospital room holding my godchild and I look over and see Claudia crying. I asked her what's wrong? She says I can't believe my daughter is finally here and my bestie is gonna be a great god mom. You are so good with kids and have that love for kids. I remember while we were sitting there talking, the nurse walked in and said, "Now Ms. Hall who is this young lady sitting here?"

Claudia said, "My bestie who has been there with me since she was 14 years old."

Now it's been a long day and I'm getting ready to leave the hospital and I say to Claudia I shall see ya'll when you get discharged from the hospital and ya'll be safe now. Now Aaliyah is headed home from the hospital in Charlottesville, Virginia and headed back to her Grandma's house in Culpeper with Claudia. I remember once they got there and settle in, I went to see Aaliyah and she was crying and her mother Claudia was like take your goddaughter and put her to sleep while I catch a nap. I was like I come to visit both of y'all and you going to sleep? Claudia said I sure am because I'm exhausted, tired, sleepy and that's what godparents do, help out. All I could do was laugh out loud. I enjoyed spending time with Claudia and her family. Our friendship got even closer once Aaliyah was born. I remember going to her doctor appointments and whenever Claudia's mom was unable to take them I would do it because Claudia didn't drive. As time went on, Aaliyah started to get attached to me and would always want me to hold her and when I would leave, she would cry. I would go visit her and she would give me the biggest smile and had a habit of throwing up on me. As the days, weeks and months went by, Claudia decided to go back to New York with Aaliyah. So, while they are in New York we kept in contact by phone because I was working at W.C. Thompson funeral home. Claudia was taking care of Aaliyah in New York. So, as days went by, I used to send Claudia money to take care of Aaliyah and get what she needed because Claudia wasn't working at the time and that was my role as her godmother. I always called to see how they were both doing and I would send stuff threw the mail or

UPS for Aaliyah, like clothes, shoes and toys. A year went by, Claudia decided to come to Virginia with my goddaughter Aaliyah. She would let me know so I could pick them up from train station or bus stop. They came down here because the struggle got a little too much. We agree for them to come here for a while then when she could get a job and get on her feet, they would go back to New York. So, while they were here, I'm still working for the funeral home and Claudia and my goddaughter would catch a ride to my job and hang out with me while I was working. When time came where I had to leave work, I would take them back to Davina's house (Claudia's mom) or sometimes they would go over to my parent's house. As time went on Claudia decided she wanted to go hang with her friends and leave Aaliyah with her mom or my mom. It was cool for a while, but then it got to a point Claudia would just be dropping her off with either her mom or my mom. They would call me and let me know your goddaughter is here and when you get off you need to come and get her. I would be like ok to both grandparents. I would be there soon as I can. So, after enough of her going out and doing her. I told her it's best you go back to New York and get yourself together because I have a job to do and the funeral home is too busy right now for me to have Aaliyah here or trying to find someone to watch her. Claudia decided to go back to New York. About roughly a month later, when she got a place and then found a job doing security work, Aaliyah is 8 years old at the time. We would barely talk because she was working and I was working and our shifts were different. From time to time I would make my way to New York to go visit them. I remember one time going up there and Aaliyah was sitting in the living room and when I walked in her eyes got so big and she immediately asked me god mommy are you staying up here with us. I told her no. I come to visit but I have to go back to Virginia later on tonight. We went out and ate and went shopping then went back to their place in New York. As we are getting close to their apartment, Claudia asked me could I stay until morning because Aaliyah had something going on at school. But by me working for a funeral home, I couldn't because I had to get back. I got a call that I had to go pick up bodies in the early morning hours. As we talked, I can see my goddaughter watching me and she said, "God mommy I want to go with you." I sat her down to explain to her you have school in the morning. You need your education and you need to stay with your mommy. I will be back when I can. Mommy will allow you to call me after school. With that being said she gave me a hug, kiss and told me she loved me and wanted me to come back soon. Now it's getting where I'm about to leave out of Claudia's apartment and I told her to take good care of my goddaughter and herself. It's also gonna be a while before you hear from me again because of my job and I had other personal responsibilities to take care of as well. She was I know and ok but you know your goddaughter is gonna want to talk to you. Months go by and I hadn't spoken to Claudia. Within that time frame, I know my goddaughter had a birthday coming up in two months so I told my mom that I'm gonna reach out to Claudia and see what she's doing for her birthday.

I called on her actual birthday and Claudia answered the phone and I said hey what did you do for my goddaughter's birthday and she said I'm doing something in New

York. I will come down the next weekend so you can do something with her because I know you want to see her. I was like great that would be good and we will do something with my family as well. As the weekend was getting close, I was getting excited because I haven't seen my goddaughter in over 6 months. Now it's time for me to go pick them up from her mom's house in Virginia. As I'm driving to the house, I get a call from Claudia asking me where am I and I asked why? She said listen and it was my goddaughter crying asking where I was. While being on the phone with Claudia, I told her to come outside because I was pulling up in the driveway. By the time I get up to garage door, I saw Aaliyah standing beside the doorway hollering that's my god mommy! She ran outside into my arms and said I missed you soo much and I want to come and stay with you. As I put her back down, I told her I will see you again real soon. Now we are going to start celebrating my goddaughter's birthday. We went to the mall and went shopping and then we went to Funland. She had a blast. Funland is a place where you can ride go carts inside, play games and win tickets and she loved funnel cakes. Now it's getting late and time has caught up on us it was time to go so she can head back to her mom's place. We headed back driving and I look in my mirror and she's knocked out. I thank her mother (Claudia) for coming down and letting me spend the day with my goddaughter. I drop them off and take Aaliyah in the house and she's still sleeping and I told everybody goodnight. Later on, the next day, Aaliyah calls me and says thank you god mommy. I wanted you to know me and mommy will be leaving tomorrow and going back to New York because I have school that Monday. I said ok you have a good week in school. After all that, I called Claudia to see how they were doing and how things were going back in New York and she told me her mom was sick and she would be coming back and forth for a little bit from New York to Virginia. Now my goddaughter is 10 years old. Why they are in New York, I spoke with Claudia barely because she had a lot on her plate dealing with her mom illness and she was working also. I had my job and I would be traveling and other things so we agree to talk as much as we can when we were able to. Months had gone by and we hadn't talk since my birthday in May. I asked her how things were going with her, my goddaughter and her mom and everyone. She said it's hard and her mom has her days but I been working and maintaining and I told her that's great to hear and keep it up. She told me she was working for a security company in New York. I asked her how she's doing. She said I'm okay and at least I'm making money to provide for me and Aaliyah to get stuff we need since you and your mom's always helping us. I going on asking her how's my goddaughter was doing in school and she said she's doing good in all. We went on just talking about old times and life in general.

Before we hang up, I told Claudia to keep me posted on her mom and that I would be gone for a while but I will check in from time to time when I'm able but give my mom a call anytime. Time has gone by and I couldn't get in touch with Claudia so I don't know what to think but I started to get concerned because I thought maybe something had happened to her or my goddaughter or even her mom. As time went by, I finally get this call from Claudia. She was screaming and crying saying my mom died and me and your goddaughter is on our way to Virginia. I'm on the other end like "Wow, OMG! Ok

Claudia just breath and calm down because you have to get it together because you have Aaliyah watching you and probably scared to death. I know you hurting but try and calm down so you can explain to Aaliyah about what just happened and I will meet y'all either at train station in Culpeper or at your mom's house." After all that we hung up and I left the funeral home to go home and get myself together so when Claudia call me back I would be ready to go get them so in the meantime my phone rings again and it's Claudia on the other end still crying but she had calmed down a little so we could talk.   In the midst of the conversation we were having, I remember telling my best friend ride of die that your momma has fought the good fight and she's now pain free and NO MORE suffering. I told her you gonna be strong for your daughter as well as your sister RiRi. I told her think of the memories you shared with your mom and know I'm here for you ALL. As we are about to hang up the phone, I told her God makes no mistakes but know God will see you through. Later on, in the day, I get a phone call from Claudia saying we here and I said, where are you? She said at train station waiting on you. Why we on the phone, I'm driving headed to pick them up and as I pull up to train station Aaliyah spots me and ran into my arms as Claudia is coming towards us with tears running down her face. We all in the car and Claudia's still crying and we are headed to her mom's house. As we pull up to the house, I tell Claudia that I'm gonna drop y'all off to spend time with your family and you can call me later and I will come back to be with you all. Claudia really didn't want me and my mom to leave but I told her it's time for you to go in there and be with your family and especially with your daughter and sister because they both need you as well as you need them. My mom said yes, we will come back and get y'all. She finally said ok and I will call you later on. So later on, that night Claudia calls and asked me to come back up to the house after I get off work because she said my mom told her to come over so they could chat a little bit. I went up there after I got off from work. When I get there, she came out to the car with Aaliyah and we sat there a little bit in the driveway then we left to go to Walmart in Culpeper and got Aaliyah something, then we went to see my mom. We went in and talked to my mom for a little bit and Claudia and my mom talked about her mom for a little bit then Claudia told my mom she was headed back to her mom's place so she could take Aaliyah to be with her sister RiRi. Now we are back at Claudia's mom's house and Claudia took Aaliyah in the house then came back out so we could talk and she wanted to talk about her mom. Claudia was saying how she missed her then asked me would I be able to attend the service when they get the arrangements together. I told her yes. Then after we talked a while, time flew by and it was almost the next day and I told her I would be in touch.

Now it's time for the wake of her mother Davina Hall. I'm standing outside in front of the church waiting for Claudia and Aaliyah to arrive. Now I see them coming across the street together and Claudia is crying so as they approach me, I told her we are about to go inside the church and I told her I'm gonna have my goddaughter with me so you can go view your mom body. Now we are sitting on the side and she is up there with her mom and all. I can see and remember Claudia screaming, crying and trying to get into casket with her. The scene just tore me to pieces.

I'm in the back with my goddaughter and I look over to her and said, "Do you want to go up there with your mom?"

She said, "No I'm gonna sit right here with you god mommy."

So, we did while Claudia had her moment. Finally, I had to wind up going up there because she was taking it soo hard and get her and take her outside for some fresh air. We are outside talking and stuff and I told her you got to be strong bestie and get it together because Aaliyah is getting scared. After all that, the service was about to end and I told Aaliyah and Claudia that y'all go ahead and catch up with your family. I will come back once I go home and change because I was in my work clothes. Well I was taking too long and Claudia called all upset and said bestie I need to talk to you. Can you come because I can't do this and I miss my mom ALOT. I get up there and before I could get out the car good enough, she ran, hugged me and said bestie I miss my mom soo much and I can't live without her. I told her you have Aaliyah to think about and she said I know but I miss my mommy so much. All I can say is I'm here for you. Pray and stay strong.   Honestly, she wasn't hearing me and I truly understood it but I really didn't know what to say because I don't know how she really felt because my mom is still living. All I know is she didn't want to be here NO MORE.   She is missing her mom bad and her mind was made up.   Claudia just kept saying bestie I want my mommy; I want my mommy and why she had to die? We talked until it was time for them to head to North Carolina to lay her mother to rest. I told her I was unable to go with her because I had to go to work and I would be in touch. She was upset but I told I have a job to do so after that I went to give my goddaughter a kiss and told her I loved her and I see her soon. As I leave, Claudia calls me and we start talking. I talk to her from the time she left Virginia until she got to North Carolina and then we hung up the phone. A couple of weeks after her mom is buried, she calls to ask me to help with my goddaughter cause she's still taking it hard, missing her mom, wants her mom, and she has nothing to live for. At this point I told her your daughter needs you and you got to pull it together and be there for your daughter. Then she got mad and hung up the phone. I left her alone and let her get herself together and think about it for a while. Now it's a month and ½ after we talk. I get this call from my goddaughter saying my mommy isn't acting right and she wants her mommy. I told her Claudia has to be strong for you and your grandmother is gonna watch over you both. My goddaughter kept saying I miss my grandma and I want to see her. I tried to explain to her that Grandma is your angel and she said, "ok god mommy."

I asked her to put her mommy on the phone so I could speak to her and she did. Claudia gets on the phone and I asked her how she's is doing and she said bestie I just wanted my mommy back. I told her I hear you but your mom is in heaven looking down on you and watching you. She said I hear you but I'm hurting and can't live anymore and I told her don't talk like that because my goddaughter needs you as well as your sister RiRI. She said ok bestie but I'm going to go lay down and I will talk to you later. The next time we spoke was days before Christmas. It was a normal conversation and she just kept saying she miss her mommy and want her back.

Before we hung up the phone, she said, "Bestie you make sure you always be in touch with your goddaughter and me." I told her for sure and I will always. I called them both the next day and my goddaughter was playing and Claudia was just chillin'. I told her I was just calling while I was on a little break and I wanted to make sure they were doing ok and I'm here for you and she said bestie I know but I just want my mommy. We said to each other we would talk soon. As time went by, I hadn't heard from Claudia and I was wondering why I hadn't heard anything. I went to work and came home and went to sleep. The day went by and I got up to get myself together and I received a phone call from my sister asking me where am I. I told her home and she said ok.

I asked her, "why?"

She said I'm coming over and I said ok. Now my sister is coming through the door crying and I asked her what's wrong she said sit down. I have some bad news. I'm looking like what? She said your best friend Claudia, your goddaughter Aaliyah's mother has been killed. I said "DO WHAT!?"

She said Claudia was found dead and murdered bad. I remember going off and crying and asking my sister are you sure and she was like, yes sis.

She has been murdered and I said where's Aaliyah at? At the time they didn't know. Man, I was just too through and didn't know what to say. I sat down on couch with tears coming down my face. All I could think about was the conversation we had since her mom passed that she wanted her mommy, she missed her, couldn't live without her and wanted to see her mommy's face. I was just blown away and couldn't believe my bestie was gone. I asked my sister why and what happened? She just told me all we know is that your best friend Claudia was murdered and sat on fire. I was so frustrated, hurt, confused, and wanted to know exactly what happen to her and if my goddaughter is ok.

As days went by, I reached out to her sister RiRi and all I could do was cry and tell her I can't believe this and is it really true? She said yes, my sister is gone. I ran into Jermaine and he was telling me that Claudia was gone and she was murdered. I just couldn't believe this happened. Now I'm trying to find out how my goddaughter is doing and where she is at. I called her Aunt RiRi and asked her where is Aaliyah? She told me Aaliyah was staying in New York with her Grandma Lora. I immediately work on trying to get in touch with Aaliyah's Grandma Lora. Finally, I was able to get her telephone number and I reached out to her asking how Aaliyah was doing and things. After that conversation, we exchanged telephone numbers. She kept in touch with me and letting me know how my goddaughter was doing. I had a chance to speak to my goddaughter and she was just saying I miss my mommy and I just want her here with me. I was so lost for words and couldn't get myself together on the phone to even comfort my goddaughter. I told her I missed her mommy too and I love her and she was my best friend. After we talk for a little bit, I asked her to put her Grandma back on the phone and I asked her Grandma to please let me know if my goddaughter needs anything. I thanked her for taking my goddaughter and for being there for her. As I wrapped the conversation, I couldn't even say nothing else but yes ma'am and we will be in touch. As I end my chapter up, I was just in shock and lost for words because I couldn't believe my bestie was gone and somebody would do that to her. As I end this,

I leave to say my bestie "Claudia K. Hall" continue to Rest In Peace, my best friend and I will love always. Your best friend and ride or die chick, Tina...

Chapter 7
Life Now and Moving Forward

My Great Grandparents, Ora and Dan Hall were my everything. They were the sweetest people I ever met. Grandma was an elementary school teacher in Brooklyn. Grandpa was in the Army after retirement. They went back home to their original home in Gates County, NC.

My Grandpa had the prettiest now white hair with curls. I used to love to play in his hair. He always gave me the biggest smile. He and Grandma had been together they were 15 years old. They had 4 kids, 2 girls and 2 boys. The youngest died at 2 from the flu because back then there wasn't a lot of medicines to treat the flu like it is now.

Grandma and Grandpa had it rough because they lost all 4 of their kids and 1 grandchild. They outlived all of these children. The 1 grandchild was my mom who died by a horrible murder.

Grandma loved her garden. She planted watermelon, green beans, peas and other vegetables.

I would always ride the tractor with Grandpa up to the garden to get more things to peel so Grandma could cook. Oh, how Grandma loved to cook. She loved to cook and I loved eating everything she cooked.

When I came down from New York for the Holidays and as she got older, she was sick with Alzheimer's, she began to forget things.

She started calling me Aunt RiRi or Kiki which was my mommy's nickname. I knew she was sick and getting worse because there is not cure.

A few years later, Grandpa started getting sick and had to go to a nursing home. He was 92 at the time. I didn't go and see him as I should have in the because I didn't want to see him like that. It hurt me to see them not able to do things that they used to do and that they loved dearly.

Once Grandpa had his stroke, everything went downhill after that. On December 6, he died. We had his funeral in Gates County, NC. I didn't make the funeral because it was just too much.

My Grandma died from Cancer. My mom was murdered a month after that. Then my Uncle AG who had Sickle Cell Disease Died two months after my mom.

Now Grandpa is gone. That was a lot and I couldn't do it. I know after all of these losses Grandma still stood by everyone's side but once Grandpa was gone, a part of her went too. She lost the person she had been with all of her life and all of her children too. She was a strong woman and a fight but two years later, Grandma died at the age of 86.

I made to Grandma's funeral because she was the last one to go. I wanted to be there. It's just really me and Aunt RiRi, her 2 kids and her husband and her dad.

I'm now 25 years old. I currently have my own hair business making custom wigs with custom coloring.

For more information visit www.aaliyahgynnisehairco.net.

I'm going to school for Cosmetology and should get my license soon. I hope to open a shop very soon.

I've had this question asked my concerning the book. The question was, "Why do you want to write a book now?"

Why? Because I have a story to tell and I want the world to know my story.

I wanted to tell the world that no matter what you go through don't let it break you. Keep pushing. Strive for the best. If I can get through all of my seasons of losses, you can too.

Aaliyah G. Hall.